CW00816276

A GUIDE TO
THE TYLER'S WORK

Duncan Adams

A GUIDE TO
THE TYLER'S WORK

Duncan Adams

Lewis Masonic

First published 1990
This impression 2008

ISBN 978 0 85318 172 9

Published by Lewis Masonic

an imprint of Ian Allan Publishing Ltd, Hersham,
Surrey KT12 4RG.
Printed in England.

Visit the Lewis Masonic web site at: www.lewismasonic.com

British Library Cataloguing in Publication Data
Adams, Duncan
1. Great Britain. Freemasons: Tylers Duties — Manuals
I. Title
366'.1
ISBN 978 0 85318 172 9

THE TYLER'S WORK

By

Duncan Adams

CONTENTS

THE TYLER'S WORK

THE TYLER'S WORK

Introduction

HIS IS an entirely different type of ritual guidance manual, aimed at assisting the officer to understand his existing ritual book more fully, and as an aid to learning. It is taken for granted that the Lodge will have adopted one of the standard working rituals, and that the Tyler will be equipped with a copy of the same ritual.

The problem commonly encountered, especially by junior officers, is in extricating their particular instructions and lines from the general format of the working. The purpose of this book is to do it for them; it is no substitute for the complete ritual book - but will be found to be an invaluable aid.

It has been said, probably truthfully, that no two lodges work exactly the same ceremonies. How many times has the junior officer said at practice, with considerable dismay, "But that's not what it says in the Book"! The result is usually a scribbled note in the confined space of the margin. No work such as this can hope to cater for every lodge's individual variations, but a sensible amount of space is left at the end of each section for the officer to make notes peculiar to his own working.

The main difference between this book and the usual ritual book is that at no point is the entire working of a ceremony printed. The reader must refer to his usual book for this information. Instead, each officer has a book to himself divided into six basic parts:-

1. General information relating to his Office.
2. The Ceremony of Initiation.
3. The Ceremony of Passing.
4. The Ceremony of Raising.
5. The Ceremony of Installation.
6. Social Board duties.

Taking, for example, the Ceremony of Raising, the reader will find full instructions for the opening in all three degrees, the ceremony itself, and the closing. This leads to much duplication, as the opening ceremony will be repeated in all four ceremonial sections. This is the essence of the book; if the officer is learning the third degree then it is all in the one place for him to study; not scattered throughout his ritual book. There are no passages lurking in obscure areas for him to miss.

There are various ritual books in use throughout the English Constitution as the basis of the individual lodge's working. This book attempts to embrace some of the more widely used versions, but does not claim to be exhaustive. They are as follows:-

1. Emulation Ritual. Referred to as "Emulation".
2. Taylor's Ritual. Referred to as "Taylor's".
3. Logic Ritual. Referred to as "Logic".
4. Sussex Ritual. Referred to as "Sussex".
5. Oxford Ritual. Referred to as "Oxford".
6. West End Ritual. Referred to as "West End".
7. Stability Ritual. Referred to as "Stability".
8. The Revised Ritual. Referred to as "Revised".
9. The Craft Guide. Referred to as "The Guide".
10. The Complete Workings. Referred to as "Complete".
11. Shakspere Lodge 1009 which, whilst not previously committed to print, enjoys considerable currency in the Province of East Lancashire.

In each section Emulation is quoted first and in full. Unless a statement is made to the contrary, it may be assumed that the other workings are identical. If there is any difference whatsoever, then this is clearly shown immediately following the area in which the difference occurs.

Throughout the book all instructions and prompts are shown in ordinary type; all words spoken by the officer are in BLOCK CAPITALS. The obligations are broken down into short lines of sufficient length for the candidate to be able to repeat.

The object of the book is *CLARITY* and *EASE OF REFERENCE*. In some areas it will be found that the references to variations within the differing types of ritual tend to cloud this clarity. *It is strongly recommended* that the reader underlines the passages which relate to his own working in red. In some instances, such as the exchange between the Inner Guard and the Tyler when the Candidate has been restored, the rituals are silent. In practice there will be some sort of an exchange taking place, but it has not been recorded - this leads to confusion on the part of the Junior Officer. It will probably be found that one of the other rituals is *not* silent, and you can underline a portion of a 'foreign' ritual which fills the gap in your own.

Many words which would normally be abbreviated have been given in full. Only the pass words, steps, signs, and penalties have been left abbreviated or totally blank. The author feels that in this enlightened age there is no necessity for creating additional confusion by abbreviating words which do not in themselves constitute "secrets'. Some confusion exists with respect to the abbreviations P. G & P.W., do they stand for "Pass Grip & Pass Word", or "Passing Grip & Passing Word"? The rule is, of course, to follow the custom of your own Lodge. However the 'Complete' ritual uses the abbreviations P..S G..P & P..S W..D, which suggest the validity of "Pass" rather than "Passing". Throughout the ritual the author has adopted this interpretation of the abbreviation. This is the only area in which the author has inflicted his personal opinions on the ritual.

Whilst the main objective of this book is to provide assistance to officers, it will also be found of great interest to students of masonic ritual. By its very nature it highlights the similarities and differences between the different workings, and sheds light on the way our ritual has developed.

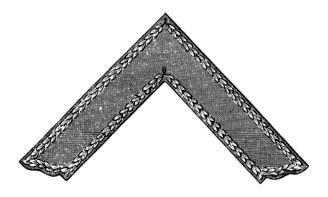

General Information

REGULATION 113 of the General Laws and Regulations of The Constitutions of the United Grand Lodge of England says:-

"The Tyler shall be **elected** by the members on the regular day of election of the Master. A Lodge, however, may resolve that a subscribing member of the Lodge shall be Tyler without emolument, in which case he shall be **appointed** with the other officers by the Master.

"In cases where the Tyler is **elected** by the members, he may at any time be removed for cause deemed sufficient by a majority of the members present at a regular meeting of the Lodge.

"Every Tyler must be a Master Mason and registered as such in the books of the Grand Lodge."

Herein lies the law relating to the appointment and removal of the Tyler. If he is elected he may be paid. If he is appointed by the Master he may not. Also it requires a special resolution to empower the Master to appoint a Tyler without emolument." Such a resolution should contain the words "that the Worshipful Master be empowered to appoint a Tyler without emolument." It would appear that the omission of the words "without emolument" on the summons will be a fatal defect.

Classically the position of Tyler is an onerous one, yet he fulfils a very important role. For this reason he often derives some financial benefit from his office.

Basically there are three types of Tyler, as follows:-

1. A brother taking progressive office.
2. A serving brother.
3. A professional Tyler.

If the office is a progressive one, leading next to Inner Guard, then the brother will inevitably be quite inexperienced. Under these circumstances the Tyler receives no financial benefit. This book should be of great assistance to him.

Many Lodges elect a brother, from amongst their ranks, often a past master, to perform the function of Tyler. He should already be well versed in the ritual of his Lodge, but this book will assist to refresh his memory. Such a Tyler will usually enjoy certain financial privileges.

The professional Tyler will often act for several different Lodges, and is invariably paid for his services. This book should be invaluable to him when he finds himself tyling for Lodges with different workings.

Whichever category he falls into, his place is outside the door of the Lodge. All the rituals agree that he is there, armed with a drawn sword, to keep out all intruders and cowans to masonry. This is his prime directive. The sword should indeed be drawn; although there is no necessity to stand menacingly at attention. It should always be near to hand, if not actually in his hand. He should, under no circumstances, wander off - to the bar for instance. This may seem like a ridiculous caution, but all too often can a Tyler be seen quickly recharging his glass while the lodge is in session.

As a general rule, whatever knocks are given by the Inner Guard on the door, the Tyler should faithfully repeat. No further mention of this is given in the following sections unless there is any variation to the rule.

It is the duty of the Tyler to see that all Brethren sign the attendance book.

A difficult situation can occur if the Tyler realises that a Brother has partaken of more liquid refreshment than perhaps he ought, and that the solemnity of the proceedings could be endangered should he be allowed to enter the Lodge. Happily the final burden rests with the Junior Warden, but you should report your suspicions to the Inner Guard who will then transmit them to the Junior Warden.

Always ensure you have some sticking plasters, rubber bands, torch, and spare pair of white gloves in your masonic case - the reason for this will be apparent in the following chapters.

The Tyler (and Inner Guard for that matter) should remember that the few lines they say to each other are part of the Ceremony, and not a private conversation. All too often is the exchange quite inaudible in the Lodge. Whilst the Tyler should not shout, he should speak sufficiently loudly to be heard by all in the Lodge-room.

It can happen that the Tyler needs to attend to some unplanned contingency which involves him making contact with someone in the Lodge (such as vouching for a late-arriving visitor). This can only be accomplished, through the Inner Guard, in an informal manner. It is common practice for there to be an 'informal contact code' such as a rapid succession of a given number (say seven) very soft knocks, or a scratching on the door. This should be just loud enough for the Inner Guard to hear. Without making any announcement he will quietly open the door and you will communicate your message. It then becomes the Inner Guard's responsibility to carry it into effect.

Whenever the Tyler is called into the Lodge, for whatever purpose, the Inner Guard will always temporarily replace him outside. In some Lodges, during the Opening, the Tyler is called in to state his 'duties'. The usual form of words is:-

"BEING ARMED WITH A DRAWN SWORD, TO KEEP OFF ALL INTRUDERS AND COWANS TO FREEMASONRY, AND TO SEE THAT THE CANDIDATES ARE PROPERLY PREPARED."

There may be some variation to this precise wording which you can note below.

NOTES

DRESSING THE LODGE

Dressing the Lodge

OU ARE RESPONSIBLE for preparing the Lodge, and ensuring that everything required for the items on the agenda is readily available. This is a great responsibility to entrust to the Tyler if he is a junior officer, and it should be checked by a more senior member - usually the Director of Ceremonies. You should ensure that you do the following:-

On the Master's pedestal place the cushion, on which should rest the closed Volume of the Sacred Law. The position of the V.S.L. should be such that when opened it can be read by the Master (Emulation working) although in some lodges the reverse applies. The closed compasses and square should be placed on the V.S.L.; the points of the compasses in the angle of the square and pointing to the west. To the right of the V.S.L. (as viewed by the Master) should be placed the Master's gavel. In some Lodges the heavy maul is also placed on the Master's pedestal. It should be noted that in some Lodges the Volume of the Sacred Law is placed in the centre of the room.

Many Lodges have markers inserted in the correct pages of the Volume of the Sacred Law to assist the Immediate Past Master to change pages when he adjusts the square and compasses for the different degrees. In such cases you should ensure the markers are correctly positioned. Different Lodges have different pages for the various degrees; if in doubt you will probably find a note written on one of the first pages. However the following are often adopted:-

1. First Degree: Second Epistle of St. Paul - reference to brotherly kindness and charity.
   Second Degree: Judges, chapter twelve.
   Third Degree: First book of Kings, chapter seven.

2. First Degree: Psalm 133.
   Second Degree: Amos, chapter seven, verse seven.
   Third Degree: Ecclesiastes, chapter twelve.

3. First Degree: Ruth, chapter two, verse nineteen.
   Second Degree: Judges, chapter twelve, verses five and six.
   Third Degree: Genesis, chapter four, verse twenty-two.

SUSSEX This ritual specifies the second Book of Chronicles, chapter six; presumably for all three Degrees.

The candlesticks are usually placed to the right of the three pedestals, but some Lodges have them on the left. In some Lodges these are lit by the Tyler prior to the Opening; in others they are lit as part of the Opening Ceremony.

Determine from the summons which brother, if any, is to attend to the reading of the portion of the ancient charges. Ensure he has a copy on his chair.

On the Senior Warden's pedestal place the level, the gavel and the column. The column should be horizontal prior to the Opening of the Lodge.

On the Junior Warden's pedestal place the plumb rule, gavel and column. The column should be vertical prior to the Opening of the Lodge.

There is very considerable variation with respect to the positioning of the Ashlars and the Tripod (if any); check the method employed by your Lodge. It may be that the rough Ashlar is placed in the north east corner, and the perfect Ashlar in the south east corner. Sometimes they are placed on the Junior and Senior Wardens pedestals respectively. If a Tripod supports the perfect Ashlar it may be placed on the Senior Warden's pedestal, or sometimes in front of it.

Ensure the stands for the wands are in position for the Deacons, the Director of Ceremonies, and his assistant. If there is to be a procession into the Lodge, the wands themselves should be outside; otherwise placed in the stands. It should be borne in mind that in some Lodges the Director of Ceremonies may have a Baton rather than a wand.

Place the Poignard on a seat by the door, in a convenient position for the Inner guard. In strict Emulation working it should be placed on the S. W.'s pedestal (if space permits), close at hand for the Inner Guard to handle.

Ensure your own sword is to hand outside the door of the Lodge.

Place the appropriate gauntlets on each pedestal. The square is for the Master; Level for the Senior Warden; Plumb Rule for the Junior Warden.

The closed box containing the working tools should be placed at a point about halfway between the centre of the Lodge-room and The Worshipful Master's pedestal. Sometimes it is placed on a plinth at the side of the Master, in a convenient position for the Immediate Past Master. As always Bro Tyler should check the particular procedure of the Lodge. Wherever it is placed it should be confirmed that it contains a full complement of tools which is:-

1. Twenty-Four-Inch Gauge.
2. Gavel.
3. Chisel.
4. Square.
5. Level.
6. Plumb Rule.
7. Skirret.
8. Pencil.
9. Compasses.

Ensure the correct columns with lights or candles are standing by the Pedestals. Ionic for the Master. Doric for the Senior Warden. Corinthian for the Junior Warden.

Ensure the books containing the words of the Opening and Closing odes (and any other material which may be sung) are distributed around the Lodge. If in short supply give preference to the most junior brethren - the Past Masters ought to know the words.

Some Lodges collect Alms during the Closing Ode, or at some other convenient time prior to quitting the Lodge-room for the Festive Board. Ensure the Alms plate (or bag) is conveniently placed - usually on, or near to, the Secretary's table.

The Minute book is usually taken home by the Secretary to be written up. However it is possible he attended to it while the Lodge was sitting, and the book was not removed from the premises. If such is the case make sure the book is on his table. In addition the Secretary should be provided with pen, ink, and blotting paper; in practice he will almost certainly attend to this himself.

The music for the Organist is probably in his personal possession, or kept in the stool on which he will sit. Ensure that this is the case; it may be your responsibility to obtain music from some other part of the building. Ensure that the organ is in working order - it may need to be plugged into an electricity supply.

Many Lodges have a particular artifact which occupies some special place in the Lodge. For example, Shakspere Lodge 1009 has a bust of the bard which stands on the Secretary's table. Determine whether or not your Lodge has any similar items, and place them accordingly.

The Tyler is responsible for laying out the officers' collars and jewels (together with the appropriate aprons if these have not been taken home by the officers concerned). There are two ways this may be done, depending on Lodge custom:

Most typically they are laid out on a table in the preparation room in strict order of seniority. If there is to be no procession into the Lodge-room they are usually placed on the chairs which will be occupied by the officers when they enter the Lodge-room.

You should ensure that the Jewels are appended to the correct type of collar; the golden rule is that all the collars should be of a light blue ribbon four inches wide. HOWEVER, if the officer is a Past Master, the collar should have a silver braid, one quarter of an inch wide, running down the centre. Again there is massive variation from Lodge to Lodge, and it may well be that the above is not observed; often an Officer will wear a collar of Office over his own Past Master's Collar. In other Lodges he will merely wear the collar of the Office despite his own personal rank. Check the custom of your Lodge.

If officers' aprons are provided by the Lodge they should bear the same emblem (a circle bearing the name and number of the Lodge, and the insignia of office) as the jewels on the officers' collars.

In descending order of seniority they are as follows:

Worshipful Master	Square
Senior Warden	Level
Junior Warden	Plumb Rule
Chaplain	Open Book on a Triangle surmounting a Glory
Treasurer	A Key
Secretary	Two Pens in Saltire
Director of Ceremonies	Two Rods in Saltire
Senior Deacon	Dove and Olive Branch
Junior Deacon	As Senior Deacon
Charity Steward	A Trowel
Almoner	A Scrip-purse bearing a heart
Assistant Director of Ceremonies	As D C with word 'Assistant'
Organist	A Lyre
Assistant Secretary	As Secretary with word 'Assistant'
Inner Guard	Two Swords in Saltire
Steward	A Cornucopia
Tyler	A Sword

Ensure that the correct tracing boards are in the correct places with the backs presented. It is assumed that the Tyler knows which board is which. Again the positioning of the boards varies from Lodge to Lodge. They are sometimes all placed in front of the Junior Warden's Pedestal, and changed as appropriate. Sometimes the First Degree Board goes in front of the Junior Warden's pedestal; the Second in front of the Senior Warden's; and the Third in front of the Master's. Sometimes the tracing boards are laid in the centre of the Lodge-room; again there is great variation, and you should check.

The warrant of the Lodge is in the strict custody of the Worshipful Master. However it is, in practice, often left on the premises. You should ensure that it is prominently displayed, usually in the north east corner of the Lodge.

The Lodge Banner should be displayed; usually in the south east corner of the Lodge.

If a ballot is to take place (which you will know from your summons), then ensure that the Ballot box and balls are to hand. The usual position is on, or near to, the Secretary's table.

The Tyler has additional duties when the Lodge is in Mourning. This can occur in three distinct ways:-

1.   By command of Grand Lodge.
2.   By the death of the Worshipful Master.
3.   By the death of a Past Master.

The following steps should be taken:-

(i).   The Secretary's table, and all three Pedestals, should be draped in black crepe or cloth.
(ii).   A black bow is attached to each of the three columns.
(iii).   Each wand has a black bow tied to it just below the surmounting jewel.
(iv).   Every officer's collar should have a black crepe rosette attached to it just above the jewel. This includes the Past Masters of the Lodge, who may well keep their collars in their own possession.
(v).   Every other brother who enters the Lodge should be furnished with rosettes to cover his normal blue ones. Three for a Master Mason; two for a Fellow Craft; and one for an Entered Apprentice. Although not entitled to a rosette, the Entered Apprentice should not be left out, and the single rosette should be worn on the underside of the flap which is turned upwards, in certain workings.

The Tyler should determine that he has an adequate supply of black crepe rosettes as soon as he hears of the death of The Master or a Past Master; certainly no later than receiving the summons which mentions the fact.

When the Ceremony is over, the Tyler should be careful to recover all the rosettes, storing them for future use.

The above represents the general dressing of the Lodge-room, but there are additional matters which must be attended to depending on the type of Ceremony being worked. These are dealt with in some depth in the appropriate chapters.

When the Lodge has been closed it is the Tyler's responsibility to ensure that all the Lodge property is safely stored away.

NOTES

CHECK LIST

In this part of the book you will "individualize" the dressing of the Lodge-room to the requirements of your own Lodge. Do this by striking out items which do not apply, inserting words where appropriate, and inserting extra items in the spaces provided. If you are a junior member of the Lodge it is strongly recommended that you spend some time with a Past Master, preferably the Director of Ceremonies, to make absolutely certain you have everything correct. If you tyle for more than one Lodge it may be helpful to purchase a copy of this book for each Lodge.

GENERAL

1. Cushion on Master's Pedestal
2. V.S.L. on cushion
3. Square and closed Compasses on V.S.L.
4. Gavel on Master's Pedestal
5. Heavy Maul on Master's Pedestal
6. Markers in V.S.L. as follows:-
   First Degree...
   Second Degree ....
   Third Degree ....
7. Columns for candles in place at right/left of Pedestals
8. Candles placed in candlesticks
9. Candles lit
10. Ancient Charges positioned at...
11. Level on Senior Warden's Pedestal
12. Column on Senior Warden's Pedestal (horizontal)
13. Gavel on Senior Warden's Pedestal
14. Plumb rule on Junior Warden's Pedestal
15. Column on Junior Warden's Pedestal (vertical)
16. Gavel on Junior Warden's Pedestal
17. Rough Ashlar placed at...
18. Tripod and Ashlar placed at ....
19. Perfect Ashlar placed at ....
20. Senior Deacon's wand stand placed at.................................
21. Junior Deacon's wand stand placed at..................................
22. Director of Ceremonies wand stand placed at ....
23. Assistant D.C.'s wand stand placed at..................................
24. All wands in stands
25. All wands outside Lodge for Procession
26. Inner Guard's Poignard placed at ....
27. Tyler's sword placed at...
28. Gauntlets placed at...

29. Working Tools placed at...
30. Hymn books distributed
31. Alms plate/bag placed at..
32. Minute book on Secretary's table
33. Pen on Secretary's table
34. Ink on Secretary's table
35. Blotting paper on Secretary's table
36. Music in place for organist, and organ working
37. Artifact ....
        in place at ....
38. Collars and Jewels laid out in preparation room
39. Collars and Jewels laid out in Lodge-room
40. Officers' aprons laid out in preparation room
41. Officers' aprons laid out in Lodge-room
42. Tracing boards correctly positioned as follows:-
        First Degree at...
        Second Degree at ....
        Third Degree at ....
43. Warrant in position at ....
44. Lodge Banner in position at...
45. Ballot box placed at..
46. ....
47. ....
48. ....

MOURNING

1.   All Pedestals draped
2.   Secretary's table draped
3.   Black bow attached to three columns
4.   Black bow attached to each wand
5.   Black rosettes on Officers' Collars
6.   Supply of black rosettes for brethren
7.   ....
8.   ....

CEREMONY OF INITIATION

1.   Declaration book placed at..
2.   Ballot box placed at...
3.   Alms plate placed at...
4.   Constitutions and Bye-Laws on Master's Pedestal
5.   Entered Apprentice apron placed at...................................
6.   First Degree tools placed at ....
7.   Poignard, near the door
8.   Hoodwink in preparation room
9.   Cable Tow in preparation room

10. Slipper in preparation room
11. ....
12. ....

CEREMONY OF PASSING

1. Fellow Craft apron placed at...
2. Square (for Inner Guard) placed at ....
3. Second Degree tools placed at ....
4. Slipper in preparation room ....
5. ....
6. ....

CEREMONY OF RAISING

1. Master Mason's apron placed at ....
2. Apron adjusted to size
3. Compasses for Inner Guard placed at...
4. Third Degree tools placed at ....
5. Sheet or Shroud placed at..
6. Emblems of mortality placed at ....
7. Past Master provided with torch
8. Two slippers in preparation room
9. ....
10. ....

CEREMONY OF INSTALLATION

1. First Degree tools placed at...
2. Second Degree tools placed at ....
3. Third Degree tools placed at ....
4. Constitutions and Bye-Laws placed at ....
5. Arrangements for collars for investiture ....
6. ....
7. ....

NOTES _____

_____

_____

_____

_____

_____

VISITORS & LATECOMERS

Visitors & Latecomers

IT IS the Junior Warden's responsibility to ensure that all masons are properly clothed, but, especially in the case of late-comers, the burden will fall on you. If the Tyler is a Junior member of the lodge, it may be very difficult to suggest to a visitor that he is improperly dressed, but if handled with tact it can save a great deal of embarrassment. Correct dress, of course, consists of dark lounge suit, white shirt, black tie, socks, and shoes and white gloves. Whilst not strictly correct, lodges vary with respect to what they allow and what they do not. You should check with the senior members of the lodge as to the exact policy.

As the Tyler is responsible for ensuring that every mason signs the attendance book, he should ensure that the host of a guest actually signs that he vouches for that guest. If a visitor merely signs that he is the guest of Brother So-and-So, you should check that this is indeed the case. It may be that the host has already entered the Lodge-room, and this may place the Tyler in a difficult position; does he permit the visitor to enter or not? This is probably a proper case for making 'Informal Contact' (see 'General' Chapter) with the Inner Guard and ensuring that contact is made with the host to confirm the invitation. It can also happen that a guest arrives earlier than his host, or his host does not arrive at all. Again the Tyler is in something of a predicament. If the Lodge is not yet opened the Tyler can ask the Junior Warden to prove the guest. If the Lodge has been opened, then informal contact may be made with the Inner Guard, and a Past Master sent out to prove him.

The Tyler should remember that his prime directive is to keep out all intruders. He can never be criticised for being over-diligent. If the Grand Master himself arrived unheralded, and the Tyler being very junior failed to recognise him, he would still be correct to have him proved. It would be a source of amusement for a long time afterwards, but he could never be criticised for it.

It is mandatory that only Craft and Royal Arch Jewels should be worn, and here you may be in difficulties. You should attempt to learn what the permitted jewels look like, and when you come across one you do not recognise, you can politely point out that it should not be worn - the wearer will almost certainly be ignorant of the fact, and you will be helping him by pointing out his error.

The only permitted Breast Jewels are as follows:-

1. Past Master's Jewel.
2. Founder's Jewels of Craft Lodges and Royal Arch Chapters.
3. Permanent Grand Lodge Charity Jewels. (May also be worn on a collarette)
4. Charity Jewels valid for the year in which they were earned.

5. Festival Jewels, unique to the Province which issued them.
6. Quatuor Coronati Correspondence Circle membership Jewel.
7. Lodge and Chapter Centenary and Bicentenary Jewels.
8. Hall Stone Jewel, worn on a collarette by visiting Masters of Hall Stone Lodges.
9. Royal Arch Chapter Jewel of the Order.
10.Royal Arch Past Zerubbabel Jewel.

Aprons and collars of officers of different lodges should not be worn in your lodge. If you are confronted by a visitor whose Master Mason's apron bears a circle with the insignia of his office, then you should point this out to him, and he should not enter the lodge with it on. This rule does not apply to Grand Officers, Officers of Provincial or District Grand Lodges and holders of London Grand Rank, and you should beware of a possible *faux pas* in this respect.

It is always wise to have a spare pair of white gloves and a black tie to lend to a brother who may inadvertently have attended without his own.

When admitting late-comers, wait for a natural break in the lodge proceedings, and then give a 'report' - usually the knocks of the degree in which the Lodge is opened.This 'natural break' may be difficult to detect; if in doubt give the report anyway - it then becomes the Inner Guard's responsibility to detect the break. Once given do not repeat it, but wait until the Inner Guard opens the door to enquire who seeks admission. If your reply is to be at all lengthy have it very clearly written on a piece of paper and do not be afraid to read from it; you should announce both name and rank. Every visitor should be named; the expression 'and other brethren' should be reserved for members of your own Lodge. Hand it to the Inner Guard so that he can also read it, otherwise he will find himself in great difficulties unless he has an incredible memory.

NOTES

CEREMONY OF INITIATION

CEREMONY OF INITIATION

Dressing the Lodge

AS WELL AS preparing the Lodge-room as described in the earlier chapter, you should attend to the following:-

1. If the Declaration Book is not in the possession of the Secretary, ensure it is placed where the Candidate will sign it. Customs vary, so find out the proper procedure.
2. Place the ballot box near to the Secretary's table, unless the ballot has been taken previously. This will be abundantly clear from the Summons.
3. Place the alms plate on the floor cloth, usually in the north east corner.
4. Place a copy of the Book of Constitutions and Bye-Laws on the Worshipful Master's Pedestal.
5. Place an Entered Apprentice apron on the Senior Warden's pedestal (or in the drawer if there is one).
6. If it is your responsibility to position the working tools of the degree: The Twenty-four inch Gauge, Common Gavel, and Chisel, on the Pedestal of whoever will present them to the candidate, then you should attend to this, ensuring they are not visible prior to the opening of the Lodge. The tools are classically presented by the Worshipful Master, but the task is frequently given to someone else - often the Junior Warden. Find out who will attend to the explanation, and position the tools accordingly.
7. Ensure you have hoodwink, cable tow, and slipper with you in the preparation room.

OPENING THE LODGE

Apart from returning all knocks on the door you have nothing to do.

Preparation of the Candidate

The Candidate should be kept in an ante-room where he cannot see either the Lodge-room, or the preparation of the Lodge members until after all have entered and the Lodge 'proved Tyled'. He should not be given the opportunity to see either the Temple or Regalia prior to his ceremony, or part of the impact of the ceremony will be lost.

Almost all candidates are nervous, even if they appear not to be. They may have been deliberately 'wound up' by friends already members of the Lodge. Without giving any of the Ceremony away, you should attempt to make the Candidate feel as at ease as is reasonably possible. Whatever you do, don't intensify his apprehension any further; it's not only unkind - it's unmasonic.

As soon as the Lodge has been seen to be tyled (Inner Guard has given three knocks which you have returned) you should begin the preparation of the candidate. Some Lodges have special items of clothing, (loose-fitting "pyjama" suits) but in any event you should ensure that he is prepared in the following manner:-

1. He must be divested of all metal, belt buckles, wrist watches, money etc. It is as well to take all paper money off him as well, or he could respond incorrectly to the Worshipful Master's request for him to give in the cause of charity. Sometimes a ring refuses all attempts at removal, use your sticking plaster to cover it so that it looks like an injury. This is, of course, not strictly legal, but where does one reasonably draw the line? Are you going to prise out his teeth fillings? What about the metal zip on his trousers? If you are tyling for a very strict Lodge it may be wise to consult with respect to an unrelenting ring.
2. Remove his jacket and waistcoat, and make his right arm bare by rolling up the sleeve beyond the elbow.
3. Undo his shirt so as to expose his left breast.
   STABILITY states 'make right breast bare' *
4. Roll up his left trouser leg to above the knee.
5. Make his right heel slipshod (usually by putting it into a special slipper provided for the purpose). It is here that your rubber bands come in useful; sometimes the slipper is too 'slipshod', and a well placed band will give added security.

6. At the last minute (see below) hoodwink him (tie a simple bow - remember the Junior Deacon has to be able to undo it easily), then,
7. Put the cable tow around his neck (he should not be given the opportunity to see it). You should ensure that the loose end hangs down his back, not his front.

* *This is sufficiently inconsistent to suggest it may be an error; there is no corresponding inconsistency in the preparation for Passing*

You need to be aware how far the ceremony has advanced so that you can hoodwink him as late as possible, and give the 'report' at the appropriate moment. In some Lodges the Secretary and Treasurer come out of the Lodge to attend to the signing of the Declaration Book and payment of dues; this is a good cue for you, and obviously your candidate will not be hoodwinked at this time. At the appropriate time you should give the 'report' on the door. Again there is massive variation as to the nature of the knocks for the report (in some lodges called an alarm), but the general form is three distinct knocks with a longer pause than usual between each knock.

THE GUIDE & STABILITY merely say the Tyler gives the report.

SHAKSPERE are very clear that an alarm rather than a report is given. It is given by making the usual First Degree knocks, waiting for two or three seconds, then giving an additional very loud knock.

The Ceremony

The Inner Guard will open the door and say "Whom have you there?"

MR ...., A POOR CANDIDATE IN A STATE OF DARKNESS WHO HAS BEEN WELL AND WORTHILY RECOMMENDED, REGULARLY PROPOSED AND APPROVED IN OPEN LODGE, AND NOW COMES, OF HIS OWN FREE WILL AND ACCORD, PROPERLY PREPARED, HUMBLY SOLICITING TO BE ADMITTED TO THE MYSTERIES AND PRIVILEGES OF FREEMASONRY.

OXFORD & REVISED: - MR....................., A POOR CANDIDATE IN A STATE OF DARKNESS WHO HAS BEEN WELL AND WORTHILY RECOMMENDED, REGULARLY PROPOSED AND APPROVED IN OPEN LODGE, AND WHO NOW COMES, OF HIS OWN FREE WILL AND ACCORD, PROPERLY PREPARED, HUMBLY SOLICITING TO BE ADMITTED TO THE MYSTERIES AND PRIVILEGES OF ANCIENT FREEMASONRY.

WEST END, TAYLOR'S, LOGIC & THE GUIDE: - MR...................., A POOR CANDIDATE IN A STATE OF DARKNESS WHO HAS BEEN WELL AND WORTHILY RECOMMENDED, REGULARLY PROPOSED AND APPROVED IN OPEN LODGE, NOW COMES, OF HIS OWN FREE WILL AND ACCORD, PROPERLY PREPARED, HUMBLY SOLICITING TO BE ADMITTED TO THE MYSTERIES AND PRIVILEGES OF ANCIENT FREEMASONRY.

IN **STABILITY:** - The Inner Guard will say "Who comes here?"

STABILITY: - MR........................, A POOR CANDIDATE IN A STATE OF DARKNESS WHO HAS BEEN WELL AND WORTHILY RECOMMENDED, REGULARLY PROPOSED AND APPROVED OF IN OPEN LODGE, NOW COMES PROPERLY PREPARED, OF HIS OWN FREE WILL AND ACCORD, HUMBLY SOLICITING TO BE ADMITTED TO THE MYSTERIES OF ANCIENT FREEMASONRY.

Inner Guard will say "How does he hope to obtain those privileges?" Prompt Candidate aloud to say:-
BY THE HELP OF GOD, BEING FREE AND OF GOOD REPORT.

OXFORD: - BY THE HELP OF GOD, AND THE TONGUE OF GOOD REPORT, BEING FREE

REVISED: - BY THE HELP OF GOD, BEING A FREE MAN AND OF GOOD REPORT.

ALL OTHER RITUALS: - BY THE HELP OF GOD, BEING FREE AND OF GOOD REPORT. *Emulation is the only ritual where the Tyler prompts the Candidate*

Inner Guard will say a few more words to you then close the door. When the door is next opened guide the candidate through it into the control of the Junior Deacon.

You will have nothing to do for a considerable period of time. Eventually the Inner Guard will open the door and usher out the Candidate 'To be restored to his personal comforts'.

You need to be aware that the Lodge is waiting for you to attend to the Candidate, and is 'marking time' while you do so. On the one hand you should be as swift as possible, but, on the other hand, you should take pains to ensure your Candidate is indeed properly dressed when he returns. His shirt should be properly fastened, tie adjusted, hair combed if necessary (it can become very ruffled during the ceremony), and he should feel quite comfortable when he returns. He should, of course, wear his new apron over his jacket, and the flap should be turned up, in certain workings (not Emulation).

While he is restoring himself you might be able to give him a quick lesson on the step and sign, these being required of him when he returns to the Lodge. This despite the fact that the Deacon will assist him when he returns.

When you are quite certain he is ready to return, give the first degree knocks on the door.

TAYLOR'S The report is a single knock.

The Inner Guard will open the door without speaking.

SHAKSPERE & TAYLOR'S: -

Inner guard will say "Whom have you there?"

COMPLETE, REVISED, THE GUIDE, LOGIC, WEST END, STABILITY & OXFORD: - are all silent as to how this is done. Follow the custom of your Lodge.

TYLER:- "THE CANDIDATE ON HIS RETURN".

TAYLOR'S:- BROTHER .... ON HIS RETURN

COMPLETE, REVISED, THE GUIDE, LOGIC, WEST END, STABILITY & OXFORD: - are all silent as to how this is done. Follow the custom of you Lodge.

The Inner Guard will close the door on you. When it is reopened guide the Candidate through it into the care of the Junior Deacon.

COMPLETE, REVISED, THE GUIDE, LOGIC, WEST END, STABILITY & OXFORD: - are all silent as to how this is done. Follow the custom of your Lodge.

NOTES ———————————————————————————

———————————————————————————————

———————————————————————————————

———————————————————————————————

CEREMONY OF PASSING

Dressing the Lodge

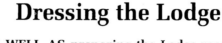

S WELL AS preparing the Lodge-room as described in the chapter 'Dressing the Lodge', you should attend to the following:-

1. Ensure there is a Fellow Craft apron on the Senior Warden's pedestal (or in the drawer if there is one).
2. Ensure a Square is placed close to the Inner Guard (so that he can present it to the Candidate when he is admitted).
3. If it is your responsibility to position the working tools of the degree at the point from which the 'presentation' will be delivered to the Candidate, then make sure that the Square, Level and Plumb-rule are on the pedestal; and that they are not visible prior to the Opening in the Second Degree. The tools are classically presented by the Worshipful Master, but the task is often delegated to another brother, frequently the Senior Warden.
4. Ensure you have a slipper outside the Lodge with which to prepare the Candidate.

OPENING THE LODGE

Apart from returning all knocks on the door you have nothing to do.

Once the Lodge has been opened, and the minutes read, the Entered Apprentices (except for the Candidate) will be requested to retire. You should ensure they do not loiter in the preparation room, to avoid them seeing the preparation of the Candidate. You should also caution them to return in about twenty minutes time.

A short while later the Candidate will be invited to leave the Lodge in order that you may prepare him. While you are doing this the Lodge is being opened in the Second Degree; as before, you have nothing to do except for returning the knocks, if required.

PREPARATION OF THE CANDIDATE

1. Remove jacket and waistcoat.
2. Make left arm bare by rolling the sleeve to above the elbow.
3. Make left breast bare by undoing and adjusting shirt.
4. Make right knee bare by rolling up right trouser leg.
5. Make left heel slip-shod, using your rubber bands if necessary for additional security.
6. Make sure he also wears his Entered Apprentice apron, the omission of which is a common error. The flap should, of course, be turned up, if applicable, but not in EMULATION.

As soon as he is prepared give THE ENTERED APPRENTICE KNOCKS on the door despite the fact the Lodge is in the Second Degree.

SHAKSPERE are very clear that an alarm rather than a report is given. It is given by making the usual Second Degree Knocks (not the First as in other rituals), waiting for two or three seconds, then giving an additional very loud knock.

THE GUIDE & STABILITY merely state that the Tyler gives the report.

There will be an exchange in the Lodge. The Inner Guard will open the door and say:- "Whom have you there?"

STABILITY: - who come here?"

BROTHER .... WHO HAS BEEN REGULARLY INITIATED INTO FREEMASONRY AND HAS MADE SUCH PROGRESS AS HE HOPES WILL RECOMMEND HIM TO BE PASSED TO THE DEGREE OF A FELLOW CRAFT, FOR WHICH CEREMONY HE IS PROPERLY PREPARED.

OXFORD: - BROTHER .... WHO HAS BEEN REGULARLY INITIATED INTO FREEMASONRY AND HAS MADE SUCH PROGRESS AS HE HOPES WILL ENTITLE HIM TO BE PASSED TO THE SECOND DEGREE, FOR WHICH CEREMONY HE COMES PROPERLY PREPARED.

WEST END & TAYLOR'S: - BROTHER .... WHO HAS BEEN REGULARLY INITIATED INTO FREEMASONRY AND HAS MADE SUCH PROGRESS AS HE HOPES WILL RECOMMEND HIM TO BE PASSED TO THE SECOND DEGREE, FOR WHICH CEREMONY HE IS PROPERLY PREPARED.

LOGIC: - OUR BROTHER .... WHO HAS BEEN REGULARLY INITIATED INTO FREEMASONRY AND HAS MADE SUCH PROGRESS AS HE HOPES WILL RECOMMEND HIM TO BE PASSED TO THE SECOND DEGREE, FOR WHICH CEREMONY HE IS PROPERLY PREPARED.

THE GUIDE: - BROTHER .... WHO HAS BEEN REGULARLY INITIATED INTO FREEMASONRY AND HAS MADE SUCH PROGRESS AS HE HOPES WILL ENTITLE HIM TO BE PASSED TO THE SECOND DEGREE, FOR WHICH CEREMONY HE IS PROPERLY PREPARED.

IN **STABILITY: -** The Inner Guard will say "Who comes here?"

STABILITY: - BROTHER .... WHO HAS BEEN REGULARLY INITIATED INTO FREEMASONRY AND HAS MADE SUCH PROGRESS AS HE HOPES WILL RECOMMEND HIM TO BE PASSED TO THE SECOND DEGREE, FOR WHICH CEREMONY HE COMES PROPERLY PREPARED.

REVISED: - BROTHER .... WHO HAS BEEN REGULARLY INITIATED INTO FREEMASONRY AND HAS MADE SUCH PROGRESS THEREIN AS HE HOPES WILL ENTITLE HIM TO BE PASSED TO THE SECOND DEGREE, FOR WHICH CEREMONY HE IS PROPERLY PREPARED.

Inner Guard will say "How does he hope to obtain the privileges of the Second Degree?"

THE GUIDE: - "How does he hope to obtain the privileges of being passed to the Second Degree?"

STABILITY: - "How does he hope to obtain those privileges?"

Tyler: BY THE HELP OF GOD, THE ASSISTANCE OF THE SQUARE AND THE BENEFIT OF A PASS WORD.

WEST END & THE GUIDE: - BY THE HELP OF GOD, THE ASSISTANCE OF THE SQUARE, AND THE BENEFIT OF A PASS GRIP AND PASS WORD.

LOGIC & TAYLOR'S: - BY THE HELP OF GOD, THE ASSISTANCE OF THE SQUARE, AND THE BENEFIT OF THE PASS GRIP AND PASS WORD.

STABILITY: - BY THE HELP OF GOD, THE AID OF THE SQUARE, AND THE BENEFIT OF A PASS GRIP AND PASS WORD.

Inner Guard will say:- "Is he in possession of the pass word?"

OXFORD & REVISED: - The Inner guard will say to the Candidate:- "You will give me the Pass Word etc." It is unclear from the text to what 'etc.' refers.

WEST END, TAYLOR'S, THE GUIDE & LOGIC: - Inner Guard will say:- "Is he in possession of the Pass Grip and Pass Word?"

STABILITY: - Inner Guard will say to the Candidate:- "Give me that Pass Grip and Pass Word".

COMPLETE: - No form of words are given, the Inner Guard merely demanding the pass grip and pass word of the Candidate.

Tyler: WILL YOU PROVE HIM?

OXFORD, REVISED, COMPLETE & STABILITY: - No corresponding words as the question was directed at the Candidate.

WEST END, TAYLOR'S, THE GUIDE & LOGIC: - TRY HIM.

Tyler, assist the Candidate to give the Pass Grip where appropriate, and prompt him to give the pass word.

ALL RITUALS EXCEPT TAYLOR'S & WEST END PROCEED TO:
★ ★ ★

TAYLOR'S & WEST END Assist the Candidate to give the Pass Grip only.

Inner Guard will say:- "What is this?"

Tyler prompts Candidate to say:- "THE PASS GRIP LEADING FROM THE FIRST TO THE SECOND DEGREE"
Inner Guard will say:- "What does this Pass Grip demand?"
Tyler will prompt Candidate to say:- "A PASS WORD."
Inner Guard will say:- "Give me that Pass Word."
Tyler will prompt Candidate to give the Pass Word.
★ ★ ★
The Inner Guard will instruct you to wait while he reports to the Worshipful Master, and he will close the door on you.

There will be an exchange in the Lodge, then the Inner Guard will open the door to receive the Candidate. Guide him through into the control of the Deacons.

You have nothing to do for a considerable period of time. Eventually the Inner Guard will open the door and usher out the Candidate 'To be restored to his personal comforts'.

You need to be aware that the Lodge is waiting for you to attend to the Candidate, and is 'marking time' while you do so. You should be as swift as possible, but you should take pains to ensure that your Candidate is indeed properly dressed when he returns. His shirt should be properly fastened, tie adjusted, etc. and he should feel quite comfortable when he returns. He should, of course, wear his new Fellow Craft apron over his jacket.

While he is restoring himself you might be able to give him a quick lesson on the step and sign, these being required of him when he returns to the Lodge. This despite the fact that the Deacon will assist him when he returns.

When you are quite certain he is ready to return, give the second degree knocks on the door.

TAYLOR'S: - One knock only.
The Inner Guard will open the door without speaking.

SHAKSPERE & TAYLOR'S: - Inner guard will say "whom have you there?"

COMPLETE, REVISED, THE GUIDE, LOGIC, WEST END, STABILITY & OXFORD: - are all silent as to how this is done. Follow the custom of your Lodge.

Tyler: THE CANDIDATE ON HIS RETURN.

TAYLOR'S: - BROTHER .... ON HIS RETURN

**COMPLETE, REVISED, THE GUIDE, LOGIC, WEST END &
OXFORD:** - are all silent as to how this is done. Follow the custom of
your Lodge.

The Inner Guard will close the door on you. When it is reopened
guide the Candidate through it into the care of the Senior Deacon.

**COMPLETE, REVISED, THE GUIDE, LOGIC, WEST END,
STABILITY & OXFORD:** - are all silent as to how this is done. Follow
the custom of you Lodge.

When the Candidate has been returned to the Lodge you should
prepare the Entered Apprentices for re-admission. As soon as the
Master has closed the Lodge in the Second Degree, and resumed in the
first (you will know by the fact you have returned the first degree
knocks on the door), you should give a report. (The Entered Apprentice
Knocks).

All the rituals are silent as to what the Inner Guard actually says and
your response; but the General format will be along one of the two
following lines:-

Inner Guard will say:- "Whom have you there?"

TYLER: THE ENTERED APPRENTICES SEEKING RE-ADMISSION.

Inner Guard will ask you to wait while he reports, and eventually he
will open the door for them.

The Worshipful Master will merely order that "all Masons be
admitted"; in which case the Inner Guard will merely open the door for
them. Under these circumstances you will, of course, not give a report.

In either case, being new to the Lodge, the Entered Apprentices will
be uncertain what is expected of them. You should have them lined up,
and tell them to wait for the Junior Deacon to instruct them as to what
to do on the other side of the door.

NOTES _____

CEREMONY OF RAISING

CEREMONY OF RAISING

Dressing the Lodge

AS WELL AS preparing the Lodge-room as described in the chapter 'Dressing the Lodge', you should attend to the following:-

1. Ensure there is a Master Mason's apron on the Senior Warden's pedestal (or in the drawer if there is one). This will usually have been provided by the Candidate's proposer. It should be properly adjusted to the size of the Candidate, otherwise attending to it during the investiture can detract from the solemnity of the occasion.

2. Ensure a pair of compasses is placed close to the Inner Guard (so that he can present it to the Candidate's breasts when he is admitted).

3. If it is your responsibility to position the working tools of the degree: the Skirret, Pencil, and Compasses on the pedestal of whoever will present them, then you should attend to this ensuring they are not visible prior to the opening of the Lodge. The working tools are classically presented by the Worshipful Master, but the task is often delegated to another officer or brother. Determine who will present them, and place them accordingly.

4. Ensure the Sheet or Shroud is conveniently to hand for laying out. It is frequently stored inside the kneeling stool. Sometimes the Tyler is called into the Lodge to attend to the positioning of the sheet during the actual Ceremony.

5. If the Lodge has a box containing 'The emblems of Mortality', ensure this is displayed, usually in the South East Corner. The torch is to lend to a Past Master to illuminate them at the appropriate moment.

6. Ensure you have two slippers outside the Lodge with which to prepare the Candidate.

Apart from returning all knocks on the door you have nothing to do.

Once the Lodge has been opened and the minutes read, the Entered Apprentices will be instructed to retire. You should ensure they do not loiter in the preparation room, to avoid them seeing the preparation of the Candidate. You should also caution them to return in about thirty minutes' time.

Likewise, before the questions are put to the Candidate, the Fellow Crafts (except for the candidate) will be instructed to retire. You should instruct them in a similar manner.

Apart from returning all knocks on the door you have nothing to do. Once the Lodge has been opened and the minutes read, the Entered Apprentices will be instructed to retire. You should ensure they do not loiter in the preparation room, to avoid them seeing the preparation of the Candidate. You should also caution **them** to return in about thirty minutes' time.

Likewise, before the questions are put to the Candidate by the master, the Fellow Crafts (except for the candidate) will be instructed to retire. You should instruct **them** in a similar manner.

A short while later the Candidate will be instructed to leave the Lodge in order that you may prepare him. While you are doing this the Lodge is being opened in the Third Degree. As before, you have nothing to do except for returning the knocks, but once more, not in Emulation working.

PREPARATION OF THE CANDIDATE

1. Remove Jacket and waistcoat.
2. Make both arms bare by rolling up the sleeves to above the elbow.
3. Make both breasts bare by undoing and adjusting shirt.
4. Make both knees bare by rolling up both trouser legs.
5. Make both heels slip-shod.
6. Make sure he also wears his Fellow Craft apron (the omission of this is a common error).

As soon as he is prepared, give THE FELLOW CRAFT KNOCKS on the door (despite the fact the Lodge is in the Third Degree)

STABILITY & THE GUIDE merely say the Tyler gives 'The Report'

OXFORD merely says 'The Tyler gives the knocks'.

SHAKSPERE are very clear that an alarm rather than a report is given. It is given by making the usual Third Degree knocks (not the Second as in other rituals), waiting for two or three seconds, then giving an additional very loud knock.

There will be an exchange in the Lodge, after which the Inner Guard will open the door and say:- "Whom have you there?"

STABILITY Inner Guard says:- "Who comes here?"

TYLER: - BROTHER .... WHO HAS BEEN REGULARLY INITIATED INTO FREEMASONRY, PASSED TO THE DEGREE OF A FELLOW CRAFT, AND HAS MADE SUCH FURTHER PROGRESS AS HE HOPES WILL ENTITLE HIM TO BE RAISED TO THE SUBLIME DEGREE OF A MASTER MASON, FOR WHICH CEREMONY HE IS PROPERLY PREPARED.

TAYLOR'S, WEST END & THE GUIDE: - BROTHER .... WHO HAS BEEN REGULARLY INITIATED INTO FREEMASONRY, PASSED TO THE DEGREE OF A FELLOW CRAFT, AND HAS MADE SUCH FURTHER PROGRESS AS HE HOPES WILL ENTITLE HIM TO BE RAISED TO THE THIRD DEGREE, FOR WHICH CEREMONY HE IS PROPERLY PREPARED.

STABILITY: - BROTHER .... WHO HAS BEEN REGULARLY

INITIATED INTO FREEMASONRY, PASSED TO THE SECOND DEGREE, AND HAS MADE SUCH PROGRESS AS HE HOPES WILL RECOMMEND HIM TO BE RAISED TO THE SUBLIME DEGREE OF A MASTER MASON, FOR WHICH CEREMONY HE COMES PROPERLY PREPARED.

LOGIC: - OUR BROTHER .... WHO HAS BEEN REGULARLY INITIATED INTO FREEMASONRY, PASSED TO THE DEGREE OF A FELLOW CRAFT, AND HAS MADE SUCH FURTHER PROGRESS AS HE HOPES WILL ENTITLE HIM TO BE RAISED TO THE THIRD DEGREE, FOR WHICH CEREMONY HE IS PROPERLY PREPARED.

OXFORD: - BROTHER .... WHO HAS BEEN RECENTLY INITIATED INTO FREEMASONRY, AND PASSED TO THE SECOND DEGREE, AND HAS MADE SUCH PROGRESS AS HE HOPES WILL ENTITLE HIM TO BE RAISED TO THE SUBLIME DEGREE OF A MASTER MASON, FOR WHICH CEREMONY HE COMES PROPERLY PREPARED.

REVISED: - BROTHER .... WHO HAS BEEN REGULARLY INITIATED INTO FREEMASONRY, AND PASSED TO THE SECOND DEGREE, AND HAS MADE SUCH PROGRESS THEREIN AS HE HOPES WILL ENTITLE HIM TO BE RAISED TO THE SUBLIME DEGREE OF A MASTER MASON, FOR WHICH CEREMONY HE IS PROPERLY PREPARED.

Inner Guard will say:- "How does he hope to obtain the privileges of the Third Degree?"

STABILITY: - Inner Guard will say:- "How does he hope to obtain those privileges?"

THE GUIDE: - Inner Guard will say:- "How does he hope to obtain the privileges of being raised to the Third Degree?"

Tyler: BY THE HELP OF GOD, THE UNITED AID OF THE SQUARE AND COMPASSES, AND THE BENEFIT OF A PASS WORD.

TAYLOR'S & LOGIC: - BY THE HELP OF GOD, THE UNITED AID OF THE SQUARE AND COMPASSES, AND THE BENEFIT OF THE PASS GRIP AND PASS WORD.

THE GUIDE:- BY THE HELP OF GOD, THE UNITED AID, OF THE SQUARE AND COMPASSES , AND THE BENEFIT OF A PASS GRIP AND A PASS WARD

WEST END & STABILITY: - BY THE HELP OF GOD, THE UNITED AID OF THE SQUARE AND COMPASSES, AND THE BENEFIT OF A PASS GRIP AND PASS WORD.

Inner Guard will say:- "Is he in possession of the Pass Word?"

STABILITY: - Inner Guard says to Candidate:- "Give me that Pass Grip and Pass Word.

OXFORD: - Inner Guard says to the Candidate:- "You will give me the Pass Word Etc." It is unclear to what 'Etc' refers.

REVISED: - Inner Guard will say to the Candidate:- "You will give me the Pass Word."

THE GUIDE, TAYLOR'S, WEST END & LOGIC: - Inner Guard will say:- "Is he in possession of the Pass Grip and Pass Word?"

REVISED & COMPLETE: - No form of words is laid down; the Inner Guard demands the Pass Grip and Pass Word of the Candidate. Presumably the Tyler assists him.

TYLER: WILL YOU PROVE HIM?

TAYLOR'S, WEST END, LOGIC & THE GUIDE: - TYLER: TRY HIM.

STABILITY, REVISED & OXFORD: Tyler makes no response as instruction directed at the Candidate.

ALL RITUALS EXCEPT TAYLOR'S & WEST END PROCEED TO ★ ★ ★

Assist Candidate to give Pass Grip only.
Inner Guard will say:- "What is this?"

Prompt Candidate to say:- "THE PASS GRIP LEADING FROM THE SECOND TO THE THIRD DEGREE.
Inner Guard will say:- "What does this Pass Grip demand?"
Prompt Candidate to say:- "A PASS WORD."
Inner Guard will say:- "Give me that Pass Word."
Prompt Candidate to do so.
★ ★ ★
Assist Candidate to give grip and communicate the Pass Word.
Inner Guard will tell you to wait and close the door on you. After a further short exchange, the door will be opened and you should guide the Candidate through to the Inner Guard.

You have nothing to do for a considerable period of time. Eventually the Inner Guard will open the door and usher out the Candidate 'To be restored to his personal comforts'.

You need to be aware that the Lodge is waiting for you to attend to the Candidate, and is 'marking time' while you do so. On the one hand you should be as swift as possible, but, as for previous degrees, you should take pains to ensure your Candidate is indeed properly dressed when he returns. His shirt should be properly fastened, tie adjusted, etc. and he should feel quite comfortable when he returns. He should, of course, wear his new Master Mason's apron over his jacket.

While he is restoring himself you might be able to give him a quick lesson on the step and signs, these being required of him when he returns to the Lodge. This despite the fact that the Senior Deacon will assist him when he returns.

When you are quite certain he is ready to return, give the third degree knocks on the door.

TAYLOR'S: - A single knock.

REVISED, WEST END, OXFORD, THE GUIDE, COMPLETE & STABILITY: - Have no form of words. The Candidate merely retires from the Lodge, and then returns.

The Inner Guard will open the door without speaking.

TAYLOR'S: - The Inner Guard will say:- "Whom have you there?"

Tyler: THE CANDIDATE ON HIS RETURN.
TAYLOR'S: - BROTHER............ON HIS RETURN.

The Inner Guard will close the door on you. When it is reopened guide the Candidate through it into the care of the Senior Deacon.

When the Candidate has been returned to the Lodge you should prepare the Fellow Crafts for re-admission. As soon as the Master has closed the Lodge in the Third Degree, or resumed in the Second (you will know by the fact you have returned the Second degree knocks on the door), you should give the Fellow Craft Knocks.

All the rituals are silent as to what the Inner Guard actually says and your responses; but the general format will be along one of the two following lines:-

Inner Guard will say:- "Whom have you there?"

Tyler: THE FELLOW CRAFTS SEEKING RE-ADMISSION.

Inner Guard will ask you to wait while he reports, and eventually he will open the door for them.

Or;

The Worshipful Master will merely order that "all Fellow Crafts be admitted"; in which case the Inner Guard will merely open the door for them.

Likewise the Entered Apprentices are returned to the Lodge when labour is resumed in the First Degree,

In either case, being new to the Lodge, the Entered Apprentices will be uncertain what is expected of them. You should have them lined up and tell them to wait for the D.C. to instruct them as to what to do on the other side of the door.

NOTES ————————————————————————————————

CEREMONY OF INSTALLATION

CEREMONY OF INSTALLATION

Dressing the Lodge

AS WELL AS preparing the Lodge-room as in the chapter 'Dressing the Lodge', you should attend to the following:-

1. All three sets of Working Tools will be presented to the new Worshipful Master. Strictly these should be presented by the Installing Master, but the job is frequently 'shared out'. Determine who will present them, and arrange for them to be in the correct places. It is possible that the Director of Ceremonies will handle this for you during the actual Ceremony. However, it is your responsibility to ensure it takes place smoothly. If you **are** responsible for positioning them, you should ensure they are not exposed prior to the opening of the Lodge.
2. Ensure copies of the Constitutions and Bye Laws are handy for the Installing Master to present to the new Master.
3. A very difficult matter to organise is the Collars which are to be used to invest the Officers; again this is your responsibility. When the Worshipful Master invests his new Officers he will need all the collars on the stand in the order in which the officers are to be invested; that is:-

Senior Warden	Level.
Junior Warden	Plumb Rule.
Chaplain	Open Book on a triangle.
Treasurer	A Key.
Secretary	Two Pens in Saltire.
Director of Ceremonies	Two Rods in Saltire.
Senior Deacon	Dove and Olive Branch.
Junior Deacon	As Senior Deacon.
Charity Steward	A Trowel.
Almoner	A Scrip-purse bearing a heart.
Assistant Director of Ceremonies	As D C with word 'Assistant'.
Organist	A Lyre.
Assistant Secretary	As Secretary with word 'Assistant'.
Inner Guard	Two Swords in Saltire.
Stewards	A Cornucopia.

The Collars should be arranged on the stand so that the Senior Warden's is the first off, and the Tyler's the last. If the Lodge is Called

Off for refreshment after the Board of Installed Masters, then there is no problem - you have plenty of time to organise it. The stand, with the collars, is usually placed to the right of the Secretary, or occasionally the assistant D.C.

If the Lodge is not called off the procedure can be quite messy, and can well go wrong. The Director of Ceremonies will probably ask the Master Masons to take their collars with them when they retire, prior to the opening of the Board of Installed Masters. Provided the stand is outside the Lodge you should be able to attend to the collars in the preparation room. Inevitably, a Past Master will still be wearing a collar and your arrangements will fall down. You need very close liaison with the director of Ceremonies on this difficult manoeuvre. By far the best solution is a brief calling off. In some lodges the collars are collected in the First Degree, and the officers thanked for the services they have rendered during the year. Under these circumstances the Assistant Director of Ceremonies will have ample opportunity to arrange them and the Tyler need not be involved at all.

In Emulation the problem does not appear to arise as the simple instruction is that the Director of Ceremonies collects the collar and the brother to be invested. In any event the Tyler is not involved in these variations, and the exact procedures adopted are beyond the scope of this book. For the purposes of the Tyler's own investiture we will, however, refer strictly to the official workings.

THE CEREMONY

Apart from returning knocks you have very little to do. First the Entered Apprentices will retire, then the Fellow Crafts, then the Master Masons. They will eventually return to the Lodge in reverse order, sometimes singing as they perambulate. If the Director of Ceremonies has delegated someone, perhaps the **new** Senior Warden, to organise them, then you can leave it up to him. Otherwise **you** should do so. If they are to sing, then make sure they have the appropriate words. The Entered Apprentices, and to a lesser extent the Fellow Crafts, will not know what is expected of them, and will be very self conscious; try to advise them all you can.

When they have all returned to the Lodge the Investiture of the Officers begins; the Tyler will be the last. This is your only appearance in the Lodge for the next year, and is your only chance to 'show off'. Many Lodges permit the Tyler considerable histrionics, and there is very great variability. You should certainly check for individual variations.

The Worshipful Master will give a rapid double knock (which you should hear).

The Inner guard will open the door and admit you.

Hold the sword in your left hand, point down, carrying collar (the ritual does not say in which hand the collar should be carried, but we will assume the left, if only because the Sussex ritual specifically says so - Emulation is silent however). In Emulation Brother Tyler salutes in the first degree with the right hand so it follows that the collar should be on the left arm

Advance to a point north of the Senior Warden, take step and give sign.

If a Past Master, Brother Tyler should advance to the South of the Master's Pedestal, otherwise to the North.

Hand Collar to The Master, lay sword diagonally across the Volume of the Sacred Law.

The Master will invest you, shake hands and sit.

Perambulate to North of Senior Warden's pedestal, face the Master, Step and Sign, retire from Lodge. Do not open the door yourself - this is for the Inner Guard to do.

This ritual assumes you are a Tyler who is not beginning a progressive office, otherwise you would not already be outside the door of the Lodge. Such a situation, which will occur whenever a different Tyler is to enter office, is left for the Director of Ceremonies to improvise. The author's suggestion is that the outgoing Tyler should enter on the double knocks as before, following the above ritual as far as laying the sword on the Volume of the Sacred Law. The Master may wish to say a few words of thanks to him for his past services. He should then salute and take a seat in the Lodge. The Director of Ceremonies will then collect the new Tyler and take him to the Master for Investiture; the ritual then proceeding as above.

Once outside the door of the Lodge you have nothing further to do except for returning knocks.

REVISED, OXFORD, STABILITY, COMPLETE & THE GUIDE: - There are no instructions whatsoever.

WEST END & LOGIC: - Apart from mentioning the two rapid gavels, the ritual is silent.

SUSSEX: - This working will be given in full, as follows.

The Worshipful Master summonses the Tyler by the proper knocks (presumably two rapid gavels - the ritual is silent). The Wardens do not gavel.

The Two Assistant Directors of Ceremonies go to the door, one remaining outside, while the other accompanies the Tyler.

Step and Sign on Entrance.

Carry sword and collar in left hand, sword point down. If a Past Master, proceed to South of Master's pedestal. The ritual is silent as to how the collar and sword are given to the Master

The Master will invest you and place your sword in your right hand point upwards.

You are escorted to the north west, with the sword at the 'carry', take step and sign, and retire. Inner Guard opens and closes door. Both Assistant Directors of Ceremonies return to their seats.)

TAYLOR'S: - Again, this working, being well documented, is given in full: -

The Master sounds his gavel, two sharp knocks, to summon the Tyler.

The Director of Ceremonies goes to the door which is opened by the Inner Guard. Tyler enters carrying sword and collar (no mention as to how), and the Inner Guard takes his place outside the door. The Director of Ceremonies closes and locks the door.

Both take step and sign, and advance to the appropriate side of the pedestal.

Tyler hands his collar to the Director of Ceremonies and the sword to the Master, who places it on top of the pedestal.

The Master Invests the Tyler, making many varied and interesting movements with the sword as he does so. He returns the sword to the Tyler, but unfortunately the ritual is silent as to how this is done and the position of the sword.

The Tyler is conducted back to the North West where he salutes the Master, and is then ushered back out of the Lodge, the Inner Guard returning to his proper station.

NOTES

THE SOCIAL BOARD

The Social Board

TRICTLY SPEAKING the Tyler has no obligatory tasks at the Social Board. The Tyler's Toast, although usually reserved to the Tyler, may be given by anyone at the request of the Worshipful Master. Indeed, in many Lodges it is given by the Senior Warden.

However, we will assume that the Tyler's Toast is to be given by the Tyler.

As usual there is great variation from Lodge to Lodge. Sometimes the Toast is given from wherever the Tyler happens to be seated. In other Lodges the Tyler will stand behind the Worshipful Master, sometimes putting his left hand on the Master's right shoulder.

The general form of the toast is taken from the third section of the first lecture and is as follows:

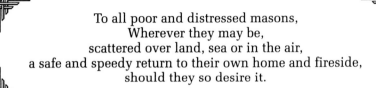

To all poor and distressed masons,
Wherever they may be,
scattered over land, sea or in the air,
a safe and speedy return to their own home and fireside,
should they so desire it.

You should then raise your glass and repeat the first line - "To all poor and distressed Masons"

There is considerable variation from Lodge to Lodge and ritual to ritual. Here are two other variations:-

"To all poor and distressed Freemasons, wherever dispersed over the face of the Earth and Water; a speedy relief to their necessities, and a safe return to their native country, if they desire it."

"To all poor and distressed Masons, wherever scattered over the face of Earth and Water, wishing them a speedy relief from all their troubles, and a safe return to their native country, if they desire it."

The last line is particularly variable; sometimes it is omitted, and sometimes expanded to 'should they so desire and deserve it'.

It is as well to make a note of your Lodge's precise wording in the notes below.

NOTES

Ref	Notes